LAKES AND RIVERS

RICHARD TAYLOR

COLLINS & BROWN

First published in Great Britain in 2001 by
Collins & Brown
64 Brewery Road
London N7 9NT

A member of the Chrysalis Group plc

Distributed in the United States and Canada by Sterling Publishing Co., 387 Park Avenue South, New York, NY 10016, USA

3 5 7 9 8 6 4 2

British Library Cataloguing-in-Publication Data:
A catalogue record for this book
is available from the British Library.

ISBN 1 85585 843 6

Editor: Ian Kearey
Designer: Alison Shackleton
Photography: George Taylor

Reproduction by Classicscan, Singapore
Printed and bound in Singapore by Tat Wei

This book was typeset using Rotis Sans Serif.

CONTENTS

Tools and Materials

This book is designed to be a pocket field guide that you can take with you as you walk around the shores of lakes or explore river banks, seeking subjects to paint. Both lakes and rivers are particularly well suited to the watercolour medium, and for this reason this first chapter is devoted to examining the equipment that you will need to take out with you to get the most out of a painting expedition.

I find that watercolour sketchpads are invaluable for working on-site, especially the ringbound types. These are light, portable and give you a hard-backed surface to support your painting. They are also available in a wide range of types and sizes. My

The sense of movement created by this jumping salmon is largely the result of the amount of white paper left untouched by paint.

Capturing Movement
Many aspects of recording water involve movement – this fish required much visual memory and a few quick notes to achieve a working sketch.

Watercolour and cartridge-paper pads are essential for outdoor use, because they are compact and allow you to keep all of your work flat and held together. They can be used for visual notes to remind you of the scene, and personal thoughts, as well as for more 'finished' paintings (which are rarely completed on-site).

personal preference is for an 210 x 297mm (8¼ x 11¾in) or 297 x 420mm (11¾ x 16½ in) pad with at least 300gsm-weight watercolour paper. This is particularly strong paper which allows a lot of water to be applied without the paper 'cockling'.

A selection of pencils allows me to make a series of quick line sketches of particular features that I find interesting. This includes B, 2B and 4B pencils, a couple of soft graphite sketching pencils, and a limited selection of water-soluble colour pencils. I find them particularly useful for making very quick studies and also for strengthening some watercolour washes and sharpening up a few lines that a brush will not always do. They are basically solidified sticks of watercolour pigment and can create a series of highly textured marks when used on watercolour paper. Their great advantage is that they can be used to sketch and then washed over with water – this turns the pigment into watercolour paint – or used as pencils directly onto wet paper, immediately providing a strong watercolour line.

Of course, it goes without saying that I also carry a set of paints, brushes and a water container. Because the painting sites with the most interest are often a fair way from the nearest car park, I find that

LIMITED COLOURS
This study of a clump of rushes used only three similar-coloured water-soluble pencils.

ATMOSPHERIC MOVEMENT
The brushstrokes used to paint water are greatly determined by the level of movement on the water.

creating a minimal painting kit is a very valuable exercise.

On location, I carry a small watercolour tin which contains a set of 12 pan paints (all colours that I have come to use after years of experimentation). The great advantage of these pan sets is that they have a ready-made mixing palette – usually the lid – and often have room for a small retractable brush. Regarding brushes, I like to carry a limited set of four: one large for underwashes and skies, one medium for applying wet washes onto wet paper, one small for applying details, usually onto dry paper, and one flat-ended or chisel-headed brush. I usually buy synthetic brushes for my outdoor kit. Nowadays, these can be a perfectly acceptable alternative to using expensive animal-hair brushes, and losing them (as I so often do) is nowhere near so annoying, in terms of cost anyway. Finally, I always like to carry a small plastic water

TRAVELLING LIGHT
A few selected pencils are a valuable asset to your sketching kit – carrying too many only complicates matters, as you have to think about which ones to use. Graphite pencils come in a variety of grades. Artists usually make use of the B (soft) grade pencils: 6B is the softest and gives rich, dark tones, while B is the lightest and offers a subtle range of greys.

B

2B

4B

6B

WASHES
When you wash plain water across marks made with water-soluble pencils, the pigment dissolves, giving the appearance of watercolour paint.

A more sketchy appearance can be created by not washing across all of the pencil drawing.

RUSHES
Some of the more linear subjects are suitable for being recorded with water-soluble pencils – these can be either washed over or left to show the pencil marks.

pot/dipper which fits on the side of my watercolour tin lid. But the one thing that you can be sure of is that you will not have any problems at all in finding water for these subjects!

Unlike many other subjects, water is fairly predictable in that it usually only flows horizontally, or falls vertically. The type of movement determines the way in which we paint the particular stretch of water in front of us, giving us very clear pointers towards the brushes and the brushstrokes that we need to employ.

Three out of the four brushes I use are round-headed, which makes them what is called 'universal' – that is, they can be used in any style for any particular subject. I tend to use them by loading a brush with paint and applying this by dragging the brush across the textured watercolour paper – this could be dry or damp, depending on whether I want broken brushstrokes with flashes of white paper showing through the stroke, or a soft bleed as the wet paint from the brush blends in with the damp paint already on the paper.

Paints and Brushes

Watercolour tins come in a variety of styles. I prefer no more than 12 pans – these colours are included in most sets, but you can buy replacements to create your own personal palette. Some tins include a brush, but you may prefer to carry a selection of you own preferred brushes.

You can use palette lids for mixing colours in.

It is a good idea to carry a small plastic water dipper in your bag, rather than taking bottles of water – you will rarely need that much to paint with. Dippers can be purchased singly from art-supply stores, or sometimes are included as part of a watercolour tin or set.

Synthetic brushes are the best type to take out on painting expeditions. Modern ones are close in quality to natural-hair brushes.

I use the chisel-headed brush for more angular subjects such as sharp rocks and boulders, and occasionally for picking out specific leaves on trees and the like.

To paint moving water, I usually employ horizontal brushstrokes, following the direction of the water across the paper. I usually work onto dry paper as this allows a few horizontal flashes of white paper to show through, suggestive of light catching on flowing water, or little crests of water as it flows and breaks along its natural path. The faster the water, the quicker and sharper the brushstrokes; the slower the water, the slower and more deliberate the brushstrokes to suggest the movement level.

To paint still water, I tend to use vertical brushstrokes. Pulling a loaded brush downwards from the river bank or lake shore onto damp paper provides a soft, gentle bleed, creating the effect of a reflection. This process can be repeated using more than one colour.

These two techniques can, of course, be combined, creating the effect of moving water in which a certain degree of reflection can be seen. The first application will need to be the loaded brush pulled downwards onto damp paper.

When this first wash of colour has dried, the second application of paint can be pulled horizontally across the paper, still maintaining the broken brushstrokes, although the highlights will not be pure white – this can be achieved, however, by scratching the surface of the paint with a very sharp point to reinstate the flashes of white paper.

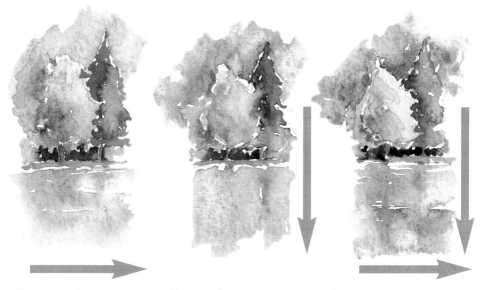

HORIZONTAL BRUSHSTROKES
These are useful to give the impression of moving water. Broken brushstrokes applied to dry paper work very well to create this effect.

VERTICAL BRUSHSTROKES
Pulling paint downwards in a vertical brushstroke seems to reinforce the effect of reflection. It also creates a feeling of quiet and calm.

COMBINATION
Combining horizontal and vertical brushstrokes can serve to create the effect of moving water which holds some reflection.

Types of Water

Wherever we find it, anywhere across the globe, the nature of water is unchanging. The way in which it flows, the ground across which it flows, and the volume of water flowing, however, are extremely variable. In fact, it is probably true to say that the natural surroundings and environmental conditions that are to be found close to lakes and rivers affect the appearance of water more than anything else in nature.

Still Water

On any reasonably large expanse of water, even the slightest breath of wind produces small ripples and a limited degree of movement on the surface – completely still water is rarely to be found in nature. There will, however, be occasions when you arrive at a lake for a painting session to find that the air is calm and barely a breath of wind has touched the water's surface.

My starting point on these days is to dampen the paper using clear water, washed evenly across the paper with a large brush to ensure an unbroken covering. I then leave the paper for a minute or two to allow the water to thoroughly soak into the fibres of the paper. As soon as the surface water has evaporated or soaked into the paper, and an even sheen can be seen on it, the next stage can begin.

It is important to make some initial judgements based upon observation: are the colours and tones reflected in the water darker or lighter than the forms that are actually being reflected, and how much do you wish to include in the composition? Having made these decisions, mix up the paints for the main bulk of the reflections and apply this quickly to the damp paper using a medium-sized brush. The paint will now bleed gently outwards, softening in tone as it becomes diluted by the damp paper. Next, use a chisel-headed brush to pull the damp paint downwards from the lake's edge to create reflections.

More colours can then be added using the same technique. The important thing to remember is not to allow the paper to dry – work quickly and decisively.

Capturing Still Water

The key to painting successful reflections in still water is to have everything that you need ready and close to hand, as you will have to work very quickly once you have applied the initial wash to the 'water area'. So mix the paints, fill your water pot and arrange your brushes.

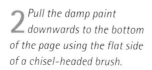

1 *Apply a line of the most prominent colour along the line of the water's edge, leaving a thin white shore line.*

2 *Pull the damp paint downwards to the bottom of the page using the flat side of a chisel-headed brush.*

3 *Add the further colours in rapid succession, and pull the paint downwards, using as few brushstrokes as possible.*

MIRROR IMAGES

Water is rarely so still that no movement can be detected at all, so it is always a good idea to allow the reflection washes to dry and then, using a small brush, paint a ripple or two onto the immediate foreground.

The same colours used for the sky, mountains and trees were used in the lake – only the damp paper diluted them. Make sure that you pull the paint down vertically using positive and decisive brushstrokes – the fewer the better.

BROKEN WATER

Gentle summer days, when breezes softly rustle the trees and boats sit calmly on the river, only occasionally shifting on their moorings, are ideal times for painting small areas along the river bank.

The basic principles that you should use for recording reflections are exactly the same as those described on pages 12 and 13 for painting still water: start by dampening the paper and then, working quickly, apply the appropriate colour wash, pulling the paint downwards with confident and decisive brushstrokes.

Once this first application of paint has dried completely, use a small brush and a limited set of dark paints to describe the movement on the surface of the water. Because the colours that you will see underneath overhanging branches, bridges, boats and so on, are actually the colours of the objects being reflected, this should be your starting point.

Choose the darkest of these colours, mix a little of your main water reflection mix to harmonize the colours, and paint a thin line that echoes the shape and direction of the ripple. Then, using plain water, wash the bottom edge of the brushstroke out into the paper to prevent a hard line forming and to give a much more natural look to the ripple. Repeat this process a few times, at all times ensuring that your brushstrokes follow the natural curve of the ripples and that the spaces between them expand towards the bottom of your picture.

For gently moving water, add the detail of the directional movement of the water only when the reflections are dry.

PAINTING RIPPLES

The key to painting successful ripples is to make some judgements about the depth of tone (ripples are often only moving reflections) and the spacing between them – not too many, and not evenly spaced. Always remember that ripples spread outwards in a rhythm, expanding as they go.

1 Create the colours by mixing a diluted version of the overhanging trees.

2 Mix the underside of the boat with the colour of the water and draw a thin line.

3 Wash the underside of the line into the underlying colour to avoid a hard edge.

WATERMARKS

Don't worry about watermarks occurring in your reflections. They can often work to your advantage, suggesting the shapes of trees and bushes in water reflections.

Use a gentle touch and select only a few ripples.

Water moves in a variety of directions, but always make sure that the ripples you paint don't overlap each other.

Moving Water

As water tumbles across rocks and boulders and breaks around them, areas of white water appear – and it is these areas of white that give a convincing impression of moving water in a painting. In watercolour, the best way to convey this is to leave areas of white paper showing as you paint around rocks and boulders. The more white paper you leave, the faster the water appears to be moving.

When you make visual notes to determine the white water, hold your pencil lightly and work with short marks. You can also scratch into dry paint with a sharp blade to create the effect of sunlight sparkling on water.

PAINTING MOVING WATER
The key to painting moving water successfully is to look at the shapes the white water makes as it breaks around rocks – it rarely, if ever, flows in a completely straight line. You may find that it helps to make a few faint pencil marks, to remind yourself which areas to leave unpainted.

1 *Fill in the background and foreground rocks and boulders, leaving the water area free of paint.*

2 *Paint the water area, leaving spaces around the boulders and several lines of water movement.*

3 *When dry, scratch off tiny flecks of paint with a sharp knife to represent light bouncing from breaking water.*

CAPTURING MOVEMENT
If you want to record moving water, try to create a 'snapshot' image of the scene in your head, and then use fluid marks to record this image on paper.

To create a feeling of distance,
space the scratched areas of
paper unevenly – closer together
in the far background, further
apart in the foreground.

Reflected shapes in moving
water appear as colours rather
than discernible images.

Fast-moving Water

The speed that fast-flowing water moves at does mean that a rapid response is required to capture the effect of movement, but this does not mean that more paint need be applied – in fact, it is the exact opposite. The amount of 'white water' found in fast-flowing rivers requires the selective use of paint and an equally selective amount of unpainted paper. The basic rule is, the faster the flow of the water, the more white will become visible as the water hits objects in its path and splashes, falls and tumbles across rocks, boulders and logs.

White water can also be emphasized as it hurtles over rocks, by painting the colours of the objects and leaving the white of the paper to represent the falling water. This involves observing closely the pattern of the falling water and the colours of the rocks and stones. These colours will usually be mixed with a combination of blues and browns, resulting in a stone-grey tone.

Painting Rushing Water

Rather than use masking fluid, use a few quick pencil marks to draw the shapes of falling water. This indicates the areas to which you need to apply paint. Apply a much lighter version of the reflected colours to paint this type of water, and paint the rocks with dark colours to reinforce the contrast.

1 *Isolate the white areas that you are going to surround with paint, keeping the colours light.*

2 *Enhance the direction of moving water by using specific and deliberate directional brushstrokes.*

3 *Use a small brush to paint the rocks and boulders over which the water is falling.*

White Water

Painting fast-moving water relies on leaving sections of paper unpainted. These areas of white are created by applying brushstrokes and colour around them. Moving water is best painted with smooth, flowing brushstrokes that reflect and echo the movement of the water.

The more white paper left unpainted, the faster the movement of the water will appear.

Painting 'behind' the white paper, leaving untouched sections showing, creates the impression of falling water.

Single brushstrokes following the flow of the water help to give the effect of movement.

RIVERS

Rivers are chameleon in character. They twist and turn as they flow effortlessly through the landscape, changing pace as they wish, and taking on the colours of the day as they go on their journeys. The colours of the landscape, the trees, the bridges and the river bank all lend themselves to the ever-changing colours of the water that flows along the river's course.

EARLY-MORNING MIST

Soft, hazy early-morning mists are often to be found sitting on the water's surface along the banks of rivers, seeming to wait for the sun to come and burn them away as the day begins.

Mist (and fog) do have physical qualities, but these are not tangible. Like clouds, they exist visually, but once inside them, they are nothing more than moisture with no apparent or discernible shape.

In the early morning mists occur above rivers and lakes as the moisture begins to rise from the water. It is, therefore, important to observe closely both the top and bottom of the bank of mist that you are about to paint. Along the base will be the water itself – the source of the moisture. There is no visible gap between the mist and the river. At the top, however, you are very unlikely to see a flat, straight line – the top of a mist bank is graduated, softly blending into the foreground colours and shapes.

Recreating this mist in watercolour requires more timing and judgement than consideration of paint and colour – success depends on how much paint you take out and exactly when, rather than how much you put on and where.

The very nature of mist lies in its soft appearance, so it is essential to avoid hard lines – carefully blot the area at the top of the mist with a piece of kitchen paper, which will partially absorb any recently applied damp paint.

The timing of this is important: if you blot very wet paper, you are left with nothing to show on the paper, but if you leave the paint for too long and the surface begins to dry, you can't remove any paint – working on barely damp paper is the key to getting this right.

CAPTURING MIST
Always try to blot along an even line, as mist does not peak and dip along its length. In addition, vary the pressure of the blot: softer at the top of the background paint, and harder at the bottom as the mist thickens.

BLOTTING
To create this atmospheric effect, gently remove the surface paint along the top of the mist with a piece of kitchen paper – use a light touch here, as you do not want to blot out the full range of colours, but simply soften the tones. Here, I painted the distant bank and the areas directly behind the mist.

1 As soon as the paint sheen begins to disappear, gently blot the top edge of the mist, removing some paint, not all.

2 Working downwards, from the base of the mist, begin to paint the river underneath accordingly.

Dark shadows and toning
on foreground trees indicate
the hard, sharp light of the
early morning.

Darker tones added
directly above the mist are
useful for strengthening
the tonal contrast.

STEPPING STONES

It can be a real pleasure to move in close to a river's edge or lakeside and observe closely the rhythmic, hypnotic movement of water running around and between stones, rocks and boulders. There are extremes of light and shade – sparkle from reflections and depths of shadows underneath large boulders – but you rarely find any extremes of colour. Paint studies of this kind thus become exercises in tonal mixing.

I mix together the cooler colours most frequently, especially cobalt blue and yellow ochre. These colours, with a little burnt umber for greater depth of tone, are an ideal base for painting wet rocks and boulders. I often dampen a rock or boulder with a watery raw sienna underwash and then apply the paint mix of cobalt blue and yellow ochre so that it flows evenly across the paper – working wet-into-wet. Before this has had time to dry, I mix a stronger version of the same colour and touch this onto the darkest part. This bleeds softly because the paper is still damp, giving a graduated appearance.

The same colours are, naturally, used for the water, although I may make several additions to allow the colours from the overhanging trees, the river bed and so on to influence the colour of the water. Observe closely the way in which the water moves and flows around the stones: the ripples that are created, and tiny pools of water that occur, can work harmoniously together as long as you don't try to put too much detail into these. Instead, suggest them by leaving just one or two highlights for ripples and a little dark paint for the reflection in the pool. What is important is to include a wide range of tones rather than illustrative or linear detail.

Even gently moving water holds shadows directly underneath large stones and boulders.

STONES AND ROCKS
These are often found in lakes and river beds. They share the same colours and tones as the water – to paint them, apply a lot of watery paint onto wet paper, allowing you to create a range of subtle tones.

White flashes of unpainted paper help to suggest the movement of water.

YELLOW OCHRE

BURNT UMBER

RAW SIENNA

COBALT BLUE

SAP GREEN

Water often flows and moves around stones and boulders – use brushstrokes to record the direction of this movement.

Start boulders with a raw sienna underwash, and then create the bulk of tones and textures using the wet-into-wet technique.

SCALE

Water itself offers no real sense of scale. We make judgements about size, depth, distance and so on by looking at the more tangible surroundings – trees, structures, boats – and here, the human figure.

A figure allows us to make comparisons between the size of distant and immediate objects that are viewed against the person. But a figure standing in the water also allows us to gauge and suggest the speed of the moving water by painting the ripples and reflections that occur accordingly. Very fast-flowing water does not allow much reflection to occur (this usually requires fairly still water), and ripples are whiter and irregular in pattern. Slower-moving water, however, allows more linear patterns to occur and a little more colour to be observed directly underneath the figure.

Finding a figure helps you to distinguish between a fast-flowing section of river, where sharp white flashes occur, and the gentler, protected sections, where the pace of the water slows and pools and ripples accumulate – rivers do not always flow at the same pace throughout their course.

VIEWPOINTS
The scale of any scene can be altered by changing your viewpoint. This sketch was made from a very low viewpoint, with the result that the canoeist's head is above the line of the trees on the far bank. This also appears to 'compress' the water, making the distance between the shore and bank seem quite small. A higher viewpoint would 'expand' the water.

INCLUDING FIGURES

A figure near the water's edge gives a sense of scale to a scene. The boulders take on a different sense of proportion, and the ripples on adopt the scale of other objects

Moving water usually holds a variety of colours.

Water flows around any object placed in it, so ripples do not need to appear as straight lines.

BRIDGES

The visual qualities of rivers and bridges complement each other particularly well. As flowing water works on old brick and stone, so the very nature of the bridge will have changed over the years.

Apart from erosion where bricks and blocks have become misshapen due to the action of flowing water, the colours and tones of the building material will also have changed. Once-red bricks and yellow stone often have a green tinge around the water line where damp has entered the fabric and left its visual mark. Equally, rich red-brick colours and softer, weather-worn stone produce some very attractive sights when reflected in the water – especially the largely untouched undersides of bridges.

Painting these scenes involves using all of the techniques examined so far. Usually, an initial wash is applied to the river area and the reflected colours are then applied to damp paper, before being pulled downwards towards the bottom of the paper. Once this has dried, you can introduce the movement of the water, either by painting ripples on top and around the bridge, or by scratching out a few sparkle highlights to suggest movement on the water's surface.

MOVING WATER
The rapid movement of water under a bridge usually holds a shadow, but does not allow much of a reflection to develop.

Bridges often cast shadows and reflections which appear darker in the water than the actual bridge.

REFLECTIONS

Look for stone and brick reflected in the water, and for light reflected up from the water onto the underside of the bridge, creating dappled shadows.

WATERFALLS

Painting a waterfall is probably one of the most daunting tasks facing any artist. So much moving water is particularly difficult to absorb visually, so I suggest that you again concentrate not so much on the water itself, but on what is happening behind it – the colours and the shapes of the rocks and boulders over which the water is tumbling.

To really emphasize the pressure of the water and the speed at which it falls, it helps to create an effective spray of water at the point where the waterfall ends – usually a pool. To create this, I use an old, clean toothbrush to spray and spatter masking fluid before applying any paint to the water area.

This gives you the freedom to wash paint freely onto the rocks behind, allowing you to create a wide range of textures as the paint bleeds, blends and dries without covering up the white paper under the fluid.

PAINTING FALLING WATER

To create the effect of splashing water, dip an old toothbrush into a saucer filled with masking fluid. Then, holding the toothbrush at the point where the spray is to be created, flick the brush head upwards – this sends tiny flecks of masking fluid splashing upwards across the paper, just as falling water does, and prevents paint coming into contact with the areas of the paper onto which it has dried. Be careful when washing paint over the paper, as over-vigorous brushwork could remove the surface of some masking fluid specks. The darker the paint, the more effective the white flecks will look in the end.

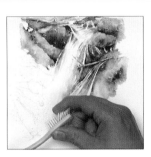

1 *Flick masking fluid upwards in the direction of the spray, using an old toothbrush.*

2 *Allow the masking fluid to dry completely, then apply the paint freely over the paper.*

3 *Let the paint dry thoroughly, then remove the masking fluid by rubbing it gently with a putty rubber.*

4 *The result is a very effective impression of spray, the white specks visible against the dark rocks.*

Little rivulets of water often seep out between rocks. Don't worry about finding their origins in your picture.

Emphasize the spray from the falling water by placing very dark colours behind it.

WATER SPRAY

The sense of movement in waterfalls is created by the white water as it falls, the spray it creates as it hits the rocks and the still water at the bottom.

LAKES

Sometimes you need to climb to a high vantage point to fully appreciate the size, shape and scale of some lakes, as their grandeur simply can't be appreciated at the water's edge. In this position it is so much easier to see exactly how the colours of the sky and the surrounding trees are mirrored in the waters of the lake.

Foreground Details

When you are searching for a subject around the water's edge, it can be helpful to include some foreground detail. This serves to break up the vast expanse of open space that often sits between you and the far edge of a lake or river, and gives the viewer something to focus on. Structures such as jetties and landing stages can add a great deal of visual interest to an otherwise dull shoreline.

In this instance, I positioned myself so that the poles of the landing stage led the eye into the picture. The mooring lines also cut across the foreground, creating even more interest in the scene.

As the foreground was the main area of interest, I painted the wash for the sky, water and background hills very quickly. The foreground was painted with more attention to detail – I painted carefully around the ropes, leaving negative shapes, and the wooden poles were painted with a combination of raw sienna, burnt umber, and a touch of cobalt blue.

The boats were accentuated by darkening the water directly beneath them with a strong mix of cobalt blue and burnt umber. As soon as this had dried, I scratched a few highlights into the foreground water to create a feeling of gentle movement.

Adding Interest to a Scene
In this picture, visual tension is created by the mooring lines diagonally crossing the upright poles. Using light and dark colours together also adds to the sense of tension: the dark colours of the wood contrast with the light ones of the water.

The negative shapes of the ropes were drawn with a double pencil line and then painted around.

Shallow water near shores is often muddy, providing limited scope for reflections: the granular qualities of earth and sand usually produce cloudy water.

SCALE AND DISTANCE

In townscapes and some landscapes we can establish a sense of space and distance by using linear perspective, focusing on key points in the scene to act as guides – fences, posts, cottages and so on. Large lakes, however, rarely have convenient features mapped out across their surface, thus removing the option of using linear perspective. This means that we have to use colour to create the sense of distance.

Distance and scale can be created by ensuring that the very furthest distance is painted with a much lighter tone, which should contain a blue or violet base. The lightness of tone helps to suggest distance. As our eyes are not capable of focusing over a very long distance, the background in any scene is less distinct, containing hardly any detail or colour.

Thanks to the earth's atmosphere, 'blue' light is reflected more than any other colour, giving the impression of blue hills or mountains when we look at wide open spaces. To create the feeling of sharp, cold lakeland days, use a cool blue – cerulean blue for example. For warmer days, a hint of violet (add a touch of alizarin crimson to sky blue) works well.

The final consideration is creating a graduation of tone from furthest background, through the large area of space in the middle, to any specific detail in the foreground. The middle ground of a lake may be only a rather vague part of the composition, with little specific detail upon which to focus. This is where colour and tone become very important. The middle ground should not be just the space in between the background and foreground, but a balance of tones that leads the viewer gradually through the composition.

You can create the distant tones by mixing the sky colour with a touch of mauve.

Distant water rarely shows any form of movement, so paint it onto damp paper to create a smooth finish.

Look for detail in the foreground only.

SENSE OF DISTANCE
To get a sense of distance on large lakes, use blues, violets and greys to complement the perspective. The soft, pale colours in the furthest background suggest distance and wide, open space, especially when contrasted with the strong foreground detail.

CERULEAN BLUE   MAUVE

SUNSETS

Sunsets are a delight to paint, but are one of the hardest subjects to attempt. First, sunsets tend to start slowly and then gain impetus quite quickly as the sun sinks behind the clouds or the horizon. You do not normally have much more than 30 minutes painting time, so a quick sketch accompanied by a few colour studies is probably the best system to develop. Second, as the sun begins to set, the surrounding landscape loses its definition as the light fades. Shadows fall upon the distant hills, and the scene becomes flattened as the colours turn to grey.

The final disadvantage of painting sunsets is the temptation to overdo colour, creating a highly unnatural scene in both sky and water. The atmospheric conditions at the end of a day can create a wealth of colours, but don't confuse quantity with strength. A collection of soft, subtle colours seen together is stunning, but they are still individual, gentle tones and hues.

The most successful method is to set a limited range of colours and to stick to them exclusively. Use exactly the same colours on the water as for the sky's colours – while they may appear different, this is chiefly because of the background against which you are viewing them.

It is very helpful to ensure that some foreground detail is available within the composition – some reeds or twigs, for example. The strength of colour and tone that can be created in foreground details as they stand against the intense light of a setting sun creates a marked contrast against the visually flattened background. Water-soluble pencils are quite useful for this, as they create a visual punctuation mark in the immediate foreground.

WINSOR BLUE

CADMIUM ORANGE

SCARLET LAKE

BURNT UMBER

PAYNE'S GREY

COLOUR AND TONE
It is best to paint sunsets when the sun is as near to the horizon as possible. This creates gentler tones and reflections on the water, eliminating the need to try to capture the full glare of a glorious sunset, however attractive the colours may be.

The sun is often lighter than the immediately surrounding sky.

Colours used for reflections are the same as those used in the sky. Paint these onto dry paper to avoid dilution.

Black does not really exist in nature. For the dark foreground, I use burnt umber, Winsor blue and Payne's grey, plus water-soluble pencils for the rushes.

Sunsets have the effect of visually flattening the back and middle grounds, so use neutral tones and a large brush to eliminate detail.

Foreshores and Beaches

On many large or even medium-sized lakes, it is very easy to believe that the foreshore is, in fact, part of the ocean – sand, pebbles and all manner of washed-up items can all be found above the water line. The explanation for this is that while they are not tidal, lakes can still be hit by storms (or even small tornadoes), which whip up waves, creating storm damage around the edges, the evidence of which is often washed up onto the foreshore.

Making paintings that include the details from lake shores usually requires a slightly different approach to composing your scene from painting rivers. Many lake scenes include, and concentrate on, a large expanse of water, and these are often painted from at least a standing viewpoint, if not higher.

If, on the other hand, you wish to include much of the appealing detritus from the weather's effect on the lake, you may need to visually sandwich the amount of water between the sky and foreground, compressing it to allow more space for the detail on the foreshore.

I find it easier to paint the foreshore and its sun, and water-bleached objects from a seated position, as this allows you to come closer to the subjects as you adopt this lower viewpoint.

Most foreshores are peppered with all sizes and kinds of stones, set into a sand or mud surface. To recreate the colours and shapes of these tiny pebbles, I use a spattering technique similar to that used with masking fluid and waterfalls (see page 30). The first stage of this process is to freely apply a yellow ochre wash to the immediate foreshore.

Once this has dried I prepare watery mixes of raw sienna, burnt umber, and usually the same blue as I used for the sky. Then I dip a small paintbrush into one mixture at a time and, holding the bristles over the dried wash, vigorously tap the metal ferrule of the brush. This sends tiny flecks of paint spattering across the paper, thus recreating the effect of thousands of tiny stones and pebbles that are resting on the foreshore surface.

On a larger scale, a toothbrush can be used. This is a much more efficient way of creating a large expanse of pebbles, as you can build up the colours and tones very quickly. It is, however, a technique that is much harder to control, and does often result in directional flicks of paint spraying outwards from the point from where you made the flick.

A combination of small specks of paint flicked from either a paintbrush or tooth-brush, plus a few selected rocks or boulders painted in with a small detail brush is often the best solution. This will provide a variety of shapes and sizes in the foreground, and will also give the painting a change of shape and tone.

CERULEAN BLUE

MAUVE

YELLOW OCHRE

RAW SIENNA

BURNT UMBER

LOG PATTERNS

Storms can easily wash up a variety of fascinating objects onto lake shores. Logs that have been in the water for a long time are particularly appealing, as they require attention to their linear qualities as well as their colours.

Sun-bleached logs need little colour: I used raw sienna and a touch of cerulean blue.

On calm days, the part of the foreshore where the water and the beach meet can become hard to define – a natural division between the land and water may not always exist.

Colours

It is fair to say that most water has little colour of its own – only the colours of mud, silt and sand that are carried along downstream. The colours that we see are more likely to be the results of reflections. The sky, the river or lake bed, the surrounding trees and rocks and boulders, all play a vital role in determining the colours that we see when we view water in lakes and rivers.

BLUES

The colours we use to paint water are mixed using the colours of the immediate surroundings – especially the sky. An overcast sky does not allow a sparkling blue lake to sit beneath it. Likewise a clear, warm blue sky rarely gives rise to a dull, lifeless expanse of water.

Certain key colours are perceived to be warm or cold, suggesting that they impart such feelings of temperature to the viewer.

These characteristics can, however, easily be altered by placing them out of context (for example, using cold cobalt blue among warm violets, oranges and reds), or mixing colours from the opposite end of the colour spectrum (for example, traditionally warm ultramarine mixed with Payne's grey and raw umber).

I don't often produce neutral colours with no temperature characteristics, as I

WARM BLUES
'Warm' skies reflected in lakes or rivers are best recorded using either of these two blues. Both are usually categorized as holding a high colour temperature that imparts a strong feeling of warmth.

ULTRAMARIINE

WINSOR BLUE

WARM GREYS
To create the base colour (that is, the first colour applied to the paper) for a river bed or bank on a warm, summer day, use these three colours, making sure that the blue is the most dominant.

BURNT UMBER

RAW SIENNA

ULTRAMARINE

WARM GREY

have rarely been out painting in neutral weather. My standard base colours can be divided into two clear categories.

For still, fairly clement days I usually mix a warm grey made up of burnt umber, raw sienna and ultramarine, and this will form the basis of my colours for water. I may well add several other colours, depending on the particular site and lighting conditions, but this mix serves as the first water wash to establish the colour temperature of the day. On days when the wind blows from the north or east, and the sky is dull and lifeless, I choose a colder grey mix as a base colour for water, made up usually of raw umber, yellow ochre and Payne's grey (sometimes with a touch of cobalt blue). I may also add several colours to this mix to help determine the exact nature of the scene and the conditions of the day.

COLD BLUES

Paint cold skies using either of these two colours. A touch of Payne's grey can be useful in either colour to reduce its blueness and introduce a more stormy sky.

COBALT BLUE

CERULEAN BLUE

COLD GREYS

A fast-running, cold mountain stream or lake often has a cold grey bed or bank. Because this usually shows through the water, these colours can be particularly helpful – but don't let the Payne's grey dominate, as this can flatten reflected colour.

RAW UMBER

YELLOW OCHRE

PAYNE'S GREY

COLD GREY

Cold Blues

The colour you choose to create a certain colour temperature is very important, as it is used for the base colour, or underwash, for most of the scene – that is, to mix the sky, the water and any surrounding hills and trees. When you are looking out at a cool, open expanse of water, search your art box for a suitable blue paint to use to paint this base colour.

In this lies one of the greatest problems that face watercolour painters – which blue to choose. Because blues are not dug from the earth in their pure state (with the exception of ultramarine, which originally came from the precious lapis lazuli, found in the foothills of the Afghanistan mountains), paint manufacturers have over the years created a wide range of blues.

While blues in general are usually considered to be in the cold end of the colour spectrum, all blue paints are individual and have their own qualities, and not every single blue necessarily imparts a cool feeling. Ultramarine, for example, is always considered to be the warmest of blue paints, whereas cobalt blue is usually perceived to be one of the coldest. Cerulean blue certainly evokes cold moods, yet it can equally be used for a fresh spring sky. Winsor blue is something of a chameleon colour and can be used effectively in either cold or warm scenes, adapting particularly well to its surrounding colours.

For this painting I used a combination of cobalt blue with a touch of Payne's grey (this colour contains black and can, therefore, easily flatten any colour) as my basic mixture and created most of the other colours using this as my starting point, ensuring continuity of atmosphere throughout the painting.

Continuity of Atmosphere
To create the water, mix the sky colour with a touch of the hill colours and a little Payne's grey. Paint the water with light sections for a high level of movement which is echoed by the sky.

The light area of water in the far distance helps to create the illusion of space and perspective.

Cold greens are created by mixing sap green with cobalt blue and a touch of Payne's grey.

Ripples are used to suggest movement created by windy conditions.

ULTRAMARINE

WINSOR BLUE

COBALT BLUE

CERULEAN BLUE

Warm Greens

The gentle, lazy lakes and rivers of summer are usually awash with reflections and the colours and tones of the warm, balmy days. Because these days create calm and placid water surfaces, the strength of the reflections, and the consequent colour of the water, is considerably increased.

To capture the relaxed atmosphere of these long, hot days spent painting at the water's edge, I tend to use raw sienna as my base colour. This is a natural earth colour which glows with warmth, making it ideal for any natural object or scene where this colour temperature is required. I often apply raw sienna as an underwash and then, while the paint is still damp, apply the other chosen colours to the trees and foliage, allowing them to flow and bleed, blending unevenly on the paper. Before these colours have time to dry, I pick up some of the wet paint and pull it downwards onto the water area, creating the basis for the lake or river and establishing a unity of colour. If you mix and apply your surroundings colours, then mix your reflection colours separately, the difference in colours is likely to show – but if you do the entire process in one go, the greater the natural effect.

A little cadmium yellow dropped onto the top of the trees serves to lift the colour a little, enhancing the notion of sunlight catching both trees and water. I also like to leave the sky until after I have painted the reflection. While the edge of the reflection is still barely damp, I apply the sky colour to the river or lake – the colours blend softly without a hard line. Once this underwash has dried, I paint on the shadows and ripples using a small brush.

CADMIUM YELLOW

LEMON YELLOW

RAW SIENNA

SAP GREEN

Create highlights on tops of trees by dropping cadmium yellow onto a wash of raw sienna and sap green.

Warm Colour Mixes
To create the warm greens of a summer day use raw sienna as an underwash, then add sap green and a little cadmium yellow. All these colours are reflected collectively and individually in the gently moving river.

Wet-into-wet reflections using all colours used on the boat were painted here, but were allowed to mix on the paper rather than being pre-mixed in the palette.

To create a variety of tones in reflections, mix sky colour and tree colour on damp paper.

Muddy Water

Muddy water is one of the few types of water that does actually hold a number of colours of its own, and is not just, visually, a product of the immediate surroundings. Still, mud-laden water can sometimes reflect the banks and branches, but to a more limited extent.

I always choose the natural earth colours to paint anything with mud – banks, river beds and water itself. These are raw sienna, burnt sienna and burnt umber for the warmer natural elements, and yellow ochre and raw umber for the colder, less colourful features.

It may seem a bit of a contradiction to say that you must take care not to muddy your colours when painting muddy water, but there is sense in doing so. If you blend a large number of the colours in your paint box together, they will invariably end up producing a bland, neutral greyish brown which does not help to describe the scene in an effective way.

For this reason, I prefer to allow my colours to mix on the paper. In this way, they do not mix so thoroughly, thus maintaining some of their individual identity. This also allows me to paint some very dark shadows onto these tones when they are dry, creating some exciting extremes, and not just a soft, dull, flat area of muddy water.

This skill of 'drawing' onto a dried underwash is particularly valuable when painting still, muddy or stagnant water. The technique allows you to create shapes and lines in a positive way, giving the reflections an added strength.

It is important that you only draw in this manner simply and quickly, and don't give way to the temptation to overwork this final stage of any painting. The sparkle from a painting can easily be lost by the heavy-handed application of too much paint or, probably more commonly, by too many brushstrokes.

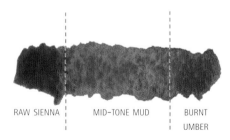

RAW SIENNA	MID-TONE MUD	BURNT UMBER

BURNT SIENNA	WARM MUD TONE	BURNT UMBER

BURNT UMBER	DEEP MUD TONE	ULTRAMARINE

Mud Colours
Choose natural earth colours to recreate muddy streams and rivers. You can create a wide variety of tones, depending on the colours you mix together.

RAW SIENNA   BURNT SIENNA   BURNT UMBER   ULTRAMARINE

MUDDY WATER

Sometimes river bed colours and sky colours combine together to produce a scene of challenging muddy colours. These can show extreme light and dark tones.

Draw reflections onto dry underwash using a mixture of sky and wood colours, applied with a small brush.

Apply raw sienna, burnt sienna and burnt umber individually to wet paper and allow them to bleed freely.

ICE AND SNOW

The long, cold days of winter can produce some very inhospitable climates – snow, ice and chilling winds are not usually friends to artists. But it really is worth wrapping up in warm clothing – fingerless gloves are a particularly useful aid – and braving the elements, as many inspiring treasures lay in wait along river banks and lakesides during the frozen winter days.

Snow is a particular challenge to the watercolour painter as it 'holds' no colour of its own. The pure, brilliant white of freshly fallen snow visually absorbs all the colours around it and reflects many of them – especially when viewed in strong daylight. A cool violet mixed with a strong quantity of cobalt blue is a particularly good colour for painting shadows cast onto snow. If mixed with some strength it can create the sharp, cold shadows of a sunlit, wintery day. Mixed lightly, it can be used to tint areas of paper to suggest soft shadows cast by snowdrifts, reinforcing the notion that daylight always creates shadows, however minimal, even when overcast.

It is important to allow the paper to act as highlights. Don't be afraid of white paper – there is no cleaner and sharper white, and if it is left unpainted, its texture can be seen, adding to the painting. The 'body' required to make white paint effective covers the texture, resulting in a slightly flat or 'dead' area of paper – in marked contrast to the rest of the picture.

FROZEN RIVERBANK
Use cold colours – Payne's grey, yellow ochre, raw umber and so on – to paint rocks and boulders surrounding a frozen expanse of water. Remember to leave flashes of white paper to act as the highlights of ice or snow.

Rather like watercolour paints, ice can be translucent, allowing the colours underneath to show through, but in a greatly more muted set of tones. Once again, I use a few flashes of white paper to represent the highlights.

The torrents of water that rush through snow-clad mountains pick up the colours of many of the stages they pass through. I often use yellow ochre in tumbling mountain rivers – it has a cold feel and suggests the silt carried along the river bed. For darker areas of tone, I add a small touch of Payne's grey mixed with a little raw umber, or even burnt umber for darker areas.

Cool violet shadows created by mixing cobalt blue with mauve and a touch of yellow ochre.

Grey tones in the water are created by mixing blues and browns in the palette.

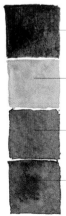

RAW UMBER

YELLOW OCHRE

PAYNE'S GREY

MAUVE

WINTER WATERFALL

Fallen snow rarely appears white: it picks up and reflects colour from the surrounding environment. The fast-moving water required a subtle application of colour to maintain the atmosphere of this winter river bank.

At the Water's Edge

The translucent qualities of watercolour paints make them particularly well suited to recording the many subtle tones that can be seen when natural objects found along the water's edge (leaves, stones and driftwood, for example) become partially submerged. The tone of the water, the colours of the river or lake bed, and the shapes of objects embedded along the shore line can all make fascinating subjects for studies.

ROTTING BOAT

Not all objects found on the water's edge are there as a result of natural erosion. This old boat had been abandoned and left to rot, and in the process had become a very visually appealing subject.

The tonal balance for recording objects like this is very important to create a sense of harmony and balance. The cool cobalt blue used in the sky, for example, was also used as a base colour to mix the faded and sun-bleached pale wood tones for the boat. I used the same blue and the wood colours (burnt umber and yellow ochre) to paint the water directly beneath the boat without adding anything else.

To paint the beach and the stones, I simply used a lighter version of the wooden boat colours, again to create a sense of unity and to keep all the tones and colours within a similar register.

WOOD
Old wood found at the water's edge often takes on a 'fossilized' appearance, making it similar in shape and tone to the rocks and boulders around it. The internal shapes may contain interesting patterns.

Use the colours of the sky and the main subject to paint foreground reflections.

Similar Tones

Always try to ensure that the tones of objects close to each other are similar – note the colours of stones and gravel on the foreshore, and those of the rotting wood of the boat.

Use your sky colour as the base colour to mix faded or rotting wood tones.

Use the same colours for objects close together, varying their tonal values according to how you observe them.

WATER'S EDGE NEST

Wildlife is particularly challenging to record in paint for several reasons – chiefly, birds' natural ability to use camouflage. Most nests can barely be seen through a web of reeds and natural protection, which means that a very limited colour palette is required, but a great deal of drawing with your paintbrush.

To record nests, create the basic tone with a wash of burnt umber and cobalt blue, working carefully around the leaves and reeds so that they appear as negative shapes in the first instance. Once this

underwash has dried, darken the centre of the nest and apply a few short, sharp brushstrokes to the complex web of twigs and sticks to suggest detail.

The assorted reeds and leaves used to protect the well-hidden nest opposite were painted a much lighter tone than the nest, using sharp, directional brushstrokes along their length. The water underneath the nest was probably the least important part of this particular study and was, therefore, painted using mainly reflected tones and with very little detail.

CIRCULAR PATTERNS
Ducks wading at the water's edge create very small ripples that radiate outwards from their feet, and these moving patterns can often be left pure white.

Suggest movement with directional brushstrokes.

Short, sharp brushstrokes suggest the rough texture of the nest bark.

SEEKING TREASURES

It is very easy to walk past some true treasures along the edge of lakes and rivers – take time to look down at your feet, and you will find fascinating and challenging subjects.

It is sometimes hard to tell where water ends and your subject begins. Allow the dark tones to work for you by creating undefined edges.

Deep tones in shaded areas visually push lighter tones forward.

SHALLOW WATER

It is not usual to witness much vigorous movement in very shallow water, especially in small pools and at the very edges of lakes and rivers, but you can usually spot a few gentle ripples which visually distort the calm, mill-pond images.

Objects viewed through shallow water are subjected to two very different types of visual distortion: physical and tonal. First, the shape of an object appears to change when part is seen on top of the water and part of that object is submerged. Second, the tonal qualities seem to change, with the section underneath the water appearing to be a little lighter. Combine these two qualities to record successfully any objects in very shallow water.

It is also important to record the concentric movement of the water and ensure that the spaces between the ripples expand as they move outwards, and that they maintain a regular shape that is in keeping with their natural circular movement.

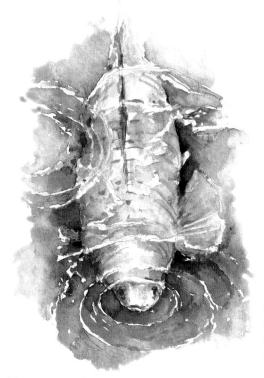

FISH IN WATER
Ensure that the area immediately beside the fish is painted a dark tone – this allows any colouring in the fish to be enhanced when viewed against a strong background, and emphasizes the lightness of the ripples.

Use a variety of colour tones, rather than grey, to paint the rocks, stones and boulders.

Create ripples by leaving plain paper unpainted.

RAW SIENNA

BURNT UMBER

COBALT BLUE

BURNT SIENNA

SAP GREEN

To create the impression of movement, use a variety of ripples – some long and thin, others shorter and a little bolder.

COLOUR AND SHAPE

Shallow water allows us a glimpse of the wealth of shapes, colours and tones found on the river bed, and the natural chaos that exists there amongst the many different-shaped rocks, stones and boulders.

PRACTISE YOUR SKILLS

Different types of water require different treatments to record them – the brushstrokes, colours and methods of application vary according to the weather and season. The projects that feature in this section are designed to take you step-by-step through the processes that I use to create a finished painting, and examine the effects of the weather on the way.

FISHING

There is rarely a shortage of fishermen along any length of river, provided that the weather is warm and the mood of the day is a lazy one.

Before starting a full-scale composition, I always make a small study or two to get the feel for a particular subject – in this case, painting the positioning of the arms and the general proportions helped me to prepare for the full-scale composition.

Next I had to make some positive decisions about the colours I would use. As the day was soft and warm, I chose to make full use of the warm colours, especially raw sienna and sap green. Both colours combine particularly well to create the lush green foliage along the river bank, and also work very well when used for reflections in gently moving water.

As both paintings were made under the same conditions, it is no surprise to find that the same colours were used in both the study and the composition – the warm greens, browns and blues that combine to create the gently flowing water on a slow-moving summer's day are as much a part of a figure study as of a larger painting. In fact, I could probably have made both the study and the painting with four paints only – raw sienna, sap green, burnt umber and ultramarine – but the tiny flashes of colour that lift the scene and add sparkle to the day required the addition of powerful cadmium yellow.

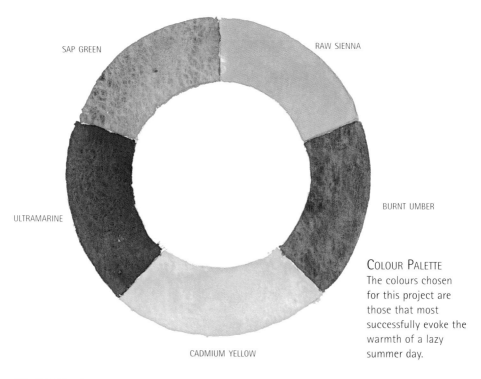

SAP GREEN

RAW SIENNA

ULTRAMARINE

BURNT UMBER

CADMIUM YELLOW

COLOUR PALETTE
The colours chosen for this project are those that most successfully evoke the warmth of a lazy summer day.

Try to make studies of figures
who look like they belong by the
water – they know that their
clothing sits easily with the
natural surroundings by using
the same colours.

Sap green and burnt
umber are good mixers
for outdoor clothing.

Darken the clothing by adding a
little ultramarine mixed with a
touch of burnt umber.

Fishing from a Jetty

The limited amount of movement on the water surrounding this rickety old wooden jetty indicated that I needed to use a wide variety of reflections when painting the water – and that this certainly included an array of greens.

I could also see from the surrounding foliage that I would need to use a lot of water to create the blends and bleeds on the paper, rather than on the palette. I employed this technique when painting the trees and their reflections in the water.

Materials

- 500 gsm watercolour paper
- Brushes – 1 large (size 12), 1 medium (size 8), 1 small (size 2), 1 chisel-headed
- Watercolour pan paints – sap green, burnt umber, cadmium yellow, ultramarine, raw sienna, burnt sienna
- Water container

1 *After making a preliminary line drawing, the first stage was to dampen the sky area and apply a smooth wash of the warm ultramarine with a medium brush. I then allowed the paint to dry to a smooth finish.*

2 *Next, I applied the base coat, or underwash, to the background tree shapes – this was a mixture of raw sienna and just a hint of ultramarine, which came from my water container as I dipped the brush into it.*

3 *Before the underwash could dry, I applied a wash of sap green to the darker-shaded areas of the background trees and allowed it to blend with the raw sienna, diluting it in the process. INSET: I then applied a touch of cadmium yellow to the tree tops.*

4 *Next I washed in the foreground foliage, and used a small brush to apply a more controlled mixture of sap green with a touch of burnt umber and a hint of ultramarine to add some depth to the tone – on barely damp paper, this ensured a bleed, but a minimal one.*

5 *I used this deep green colour mix to paint the area directly underneath the jetty, including the water. Using a medium brush, I pulled the colour downwards onto pre-dampened paper.*

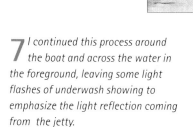

6 To develop the water tones I added a mix of burnt umber and ultramarine for the shadow underneath the jetty, and allowed this to bleed. INSET: When it dried I used the same colour to paint in some ripples using a chisel-headed brush.

7 I continued this process around the boat and across the water in the foreground, leaving some light flashes of underwash showing to emphasize the light reflection coming from the jetty.

8 When all the water had dried fully, I used the pointed section of a sharp blade and carefully scratched a few lines into the paper, removing the surface and exposing pure white to suggest highlights and a little sparkle.

9 Returning to the jetty, I used a mixture of raw sienna, burnt sienna and a touch of burnt umber to create some texture using rough, broken brushstrokes with a small brush onto dry paper.

10 Once the main colours had dried, I introduced a little ultramarine to the mixture and carefully painted a broken line directly underneath any overlaps and left it to dry, creating a feeling of recession and depth.

11 The clutter on the top of the jetty was next. I drew a few lines with a small brush to create the wooden planks, using the same mixture and technique as Stage 10, and painted the rusting can by applying pure burnt sienna onto wet paper.

12 The final details of the figure and the boat were all painted using a small brush and careful observation of shape and colour, especially on the inside of the boat, where the lighting was important to create a three-dimensional effect.

GENTLY MOVING WATER

The feeling of gentle, lazy water movement can be created by combining the techniques of pulling down paint to achieve recognizable reflections, painting a few ripples on top, and finally scratching away a few highlights to reveal the white paper underneath.

To create a more natural look, allow tones of trees and bushes to mix on the paper.

Draw details onto dry paper in the very last stages of the painting.

Mountain Reflections

The higher you climb in a mountainous environment, the sharper and clearer the light becomes, and the more you become aware of atmospheric conditions.

The one thing that was clear from the beginning with both the study and the finished painting was that I needed to use a particularly strong blue and an equally able red /mauve to tint the blue and remove any coldness from time to time. My choice was Winsor blue for both pictures. This is a very strong colour that has a tendency to stain paper very soon after being applied, making it quite difficult to blot out cloud shapes – either in the sky or the water – unless you work very quickly and blot the required shapes within seconds of applying the paint. Alizarin crimson was the next choice, to create the soft violet tones that can be seen in distant mountains. This paint is similar to Winsor blue in that a little goes a very long way, so only the slightest touch was required to take the edge off the coldness of the blue.

I also used raw umber and yellow ochre – both natural earth colours, but both on the cooler end of the colour spectrum. Although the sun was bright, casting shadows onto rocks and snow, creating very attractive scenes for both study and painting, there was little warmth to be found in the high mountains, and for most of the time the colours were used to impart a feeling of sharpness and chill.

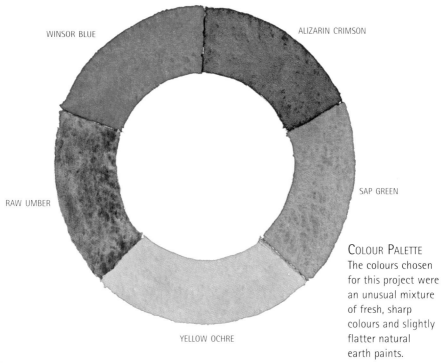

WINSOR BLUE

ALIZARIN CRIMSON

RAW UMBER

SAP GREEN

YELLOW OCHRE

Colour Palette
The colours chosen for this project were an unusual mixture of fresh, sharp colours and slightly flatter natural earth paints.

*To create a sense of
distance, judge the
lightness of tone required
in faraway objects.*

SHAPE AND COLOUR

Mirror images are rare – as
artists, we need to look for
colours and tones as well as
shapes that echo the
surrounding environment in
lakeland reflections.

Winter Lakeside

The cool, sharp atmosphere of a mountain lake is a true pleasure to witness. Painting this scene involves making a few choices about the colours you need to use, and these come largely from the cooler end of the colour spectrum – although not exclusively. You usually find a balance in nature where colours and tones harmonize: the warmer tones on the rocks and trees in the middle ground, for example, sit easily with the cooler grey colours of the snow fields of the distant mountains.

MATERIALS

• 500 gsm watercolour paper

• Brushes – 1 large (size 12), 1 medium (size 8), 1 small (size 2), 1 chisel-headed

• Watercolour pan paints – Winsor blue, alizarin crimson, sap green, yellow ochre, raw umber

• Kitchen paper

• Water container

1 *To begin, I dampened the sky area and, using a large brush, applied a wash of Winsor blue and allowed this to flow evenly across the paper. I actively encouraged the paint to accumulate at the top of the paper, leaving a lighter section along the ridges of the mountains.*

2 *I blocked in the grey tones of the mountains using a mixture of raw umber and Winsor blue on dry paper with a chisel-headed brush. INSET: I then used a small brush to intensify the stone-grey paint by adding a touch of alizarin crimson.*

3 *The shadows cast onto the snow used a very diluted mixture of alizarin crimson and a touch of Winsor blue, and I washed them out at the edges to prevent hard lines occurring here.*

4 *The middle-ground rocks and pine trees were all treated to a yellow ochre underwash to visually anchor them into the same part of the composition. This was allowed to dry completely.*

5 *I painted the middle-ground rocks using a combination of raw umber and Winsor blue, applied with a medium brush. I pulled the colour across the dry paper using broken brushstrokes, allowing the underwash to show through.*

6 *Before this mixture had time to dry fully, I pulled a little of the rock colour down onto the snow directly below to act as a shadow, tonally harmonizing the different aspects of the scene.*

7 *I mixed a little sap green with raw umber and a touch of Winsor blue to create a cold, distant blue/green, and painted it onto the middle-ground trees using a small brush. INSET: I then blotted the top areas with kitchen roll to expose the yellow ochre underwash.*

8 *This process was continued across the middle ground until the entire section was complete. I could now see very clearly which colours I would need to pull down onto the water for the reflections.*

9 *Using a large brush I dampened the lake area and, using the colours left in my palette, applied the colours (working around the snow field reflections) using vertical brushstrokes.*

10 *When this had dried, I took a small brush, mixed all the paints together in the palette, and painted on a few thin lines of ripples, moving outwards around the edge of the lake.*

11 *Once the reflections and ripples had fully dried, I scratched out a few areas of sparkle to enhance the effect of light.*

12 *The final stage was to sharpen up any edges or shadows that needed reinforcing and to make a final check that all the elements in the composition were visually balanced.*

The soft grey of the distant mountains contains a hint of violet.

The shadows on the snow are diluted versions of the surrounding colours.

BALANCE

Aim for a balance of all elements in your paintings: the warm and cold colours, and the stillness of the background and the movement in the foreground. Both sit together particularly well in this painting.

Wildlife

At certain times of the year, wild geese instinctively know that it is time they should start moving to warmer climates. This allows us the opportunity to sketch and paint them as they sit and feed, or on their graceful flight paths. While these birds gather in their flocks around the shores of lakes, we are offered a rare chance to capture them in pencil or paint as they make preparations for their annual migration. Some of the best times to witness these gatherings and flights are in the early evening as the autumnal sun begins to set, casting a gentle golden cover across the sky. To record this, apply a strong mix of raw sienna, which imparts a feeling of warmth to any scene.

As geese fly across the sky, they appear as graceful white shapes, extended as their elegant necks lean forward. To paint these birds on the ground involves closer observation of their natural colours. The grey of a goose's neck can be recorded with Payne's grey, toned down with a hint of burnt or raw umber (depending on the species), and the pure, soft white of its feathers needs only the slightest touch of yellow ochre to take the sharpness from the white of the watercolour paper.

As with all wildlife painting, suggestion is the key to success – you won't be able to paint all the feathers, so just use a few brushstrokes or water-soluble pencil marks to indicate that they are there.

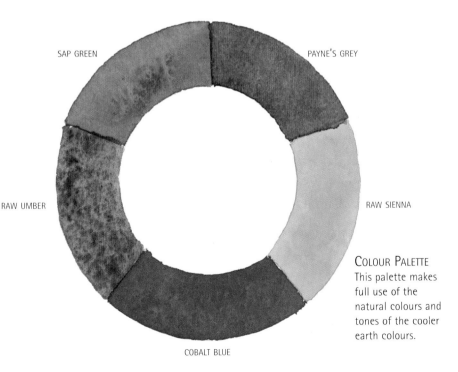

SAP GREEN

PAYNE'S GREY

RAW UMBER

RAW SIENNA

COBALT BLUE

Colour Palette
This palette makes full use of the natural colours and tones of the cooler earth colours.

To achieve a smooth finish, apply a small amount of paint to damp paper and pull it around the shape using a medium brush, then leave it to dry.

Use a small brush or water-soluble pencils on top of the underwash to suggest feathers.

FEATHERS AND WINGS

Use a medium brush and work wet-into-wet to achieve the correct overall colour for the wings, then pull some paint outwards as it dries to achieve a feather effect. This has to be done quite quickly so that the paint doesn't dry before you have manipulated it.

Flying Geese

As the sun starts to set in the autumnal sky and the shadows start to lengthen, the side of a lake is a good place to paint – and if a small flock of geese should fly past at the same time, then all the better.

In this composition, the geese appear almost as negative shapes, but this is because they are viewed against a dark backdrop that emphasizes their whiteness. This is called the push-pull technique: one colour appears to push the other forward or pull the other back.

Materials
- 500 gsm watercolour paper
- Brushes – 1 large (size 12), 1 medium (size 8), 1 small (size 2)
- Watercolour pan paints – sap green, Payne's grey, raw sienna, cobalt blue, raw umber
- Water container

1 *The first step of this painting was to dampen the sky and then, using a large brush, apply a wash of cobalt blue to the top section. When this was nearly dry, I added a wash of raw sienna to the lower sky area just above the trees.*

2 *Using a medium brush I mixed sap green, raw umber and a touch of Payne's grey and began to paint the far-distant trees with a few brushstrokes where the sky colour could show through them. INSET: I continued until all these trees had been painted.*

3 *Using a little cobalt blue instead of Payne's grey in the mixture, I painted the middle-ground bushes on the island so that they appeared a lighter tone than (and so would stand out against) the background colours.*

4 *To paint the lake, I used exactly the same colours and techniques for painting the sky, except that this was an upside-down version painted using a medium brush.*

5 *The final touches could now be put onto the middle ground. Using a small brush I sharpened the line of the beach and the water's edge. INSET: I then painted in the shadows and reflections from the far-distant row of trees.*

6 To begin painting the foreground, I mixed sap green with a little raw umber and washed this onto very damp paper using a large brush. This paint bled naturally and dried with shapes that suggested clumps of grass.

7 I strengthened the foreground underwash with a second wash, only less diluted and therefore tonally stronger. This included directional shadows from the trees.

8 Next, I treated the trees to an underwash of raw sienna, before painting a mixture of raw sienna and cobalt blue onto their shaded side.

9 *I pulled this paint around the shape of the tree, leaving flashes of underwash showing through as highlights. The few feathery sections of greenery were then painted using the grass paint.*

10 *The geese required some detail to be added on their heads, undersides and legs. I painted these with a small brush using a combination of cobalt blue and Payne's grey.*

11 *As usual, the final stage of this painting involved tidying up any loose edges, and sharpening reflections, shadows and the tiny details that can make a painting feel complete.*

MOVEMENT

The sense of movement created by these graceful geese owes much to the fact that they are being visually pushed forward by the background colours. In addition, they cast no shadow and have no reflections – tricks that artists usually employ in order to anchor objects onto the ground.

Virtually every colour used in the landscape and sky is used in the reflections in the water.

Strong tones and colours in tree shadows help to suggest the time of day.

WATERFALL

Waterfalls come in a wide variety of shapes and sizes, ranging from the smallest trickle across a collection of boulders to vast falls that plummet across treacherous and inhospitable rock faces.

The main decision to make here is whether or not to use masking fluid: although it allows you to reproduce a very effective spray, it can, if over-used, give a slightly unnatural effect to a picture.

As mentioned before, I find it very useful to make a brief study of my subject. In this case, the waterfall was not powerful enough to warrant the use of masking fluid, and I kept the white paper untouched by paint to create the effect of fast-falling water. The study maintains an element of spontaneity by my not overworking the

water. Too much paint applied to rapids can flatten them and reduce the effect of movement – the more paper left unpainted here, the more successful.

The toning that did occur on the water was created by using a lightly diluted version of the rock colours, touched on gently in a vertical direction with a small brush.

The colours used in the rocks and boulders are a combination of natural earth colours with a touch of cobalt blue (one of the cooler blues) to prevent the scene from appearing too warm, helping to at least suggest the cool nature of the water falling from this mountain stream. This, combined with the sharpness of the white paper, completes the tonal balance between the warm rocks and the cold water.

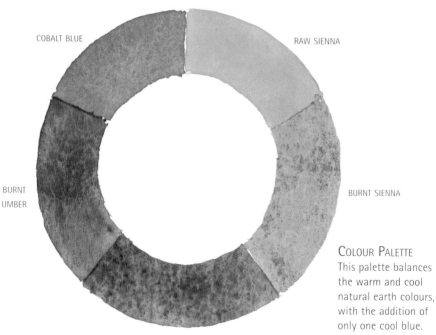

COBALT BLUE

RAW SIENNA

BURNT UMBER

BURNT SIENNA

RAW UMBER

COLOUR PALETTE
This palette balances the warm and cool natural earth colours, with the addition of only one cool blue.

REFLECTED COLOURS
Fast-moving water always reflects the colours of the rocks and boulders across which it falls and tumbles. Use few colours, but as extensive a range of tones as you can manage, to paint the stones and their colour in the water.

Look for the patterns in the water underneath the waterfall – these give an indication of the strength and pressure of the falling water.

TUMBLING WATER

Even though this particular waterfall was quite small compared with many that you might encounter, the water was tumbling across the rocks and boulders with enough force to create a series of large splashes as little droplets of water flew outwards across the scene.

It soon became clear that – unlike the study I had made – this scene would need the use of masking fluid if I were to produce a painting that did it justice, and that it would have to be applied vigorously to create the best effect.

MATERIALS
- 500 gsm watercolour paper
- Brushes – 1 large (size 12), 1 medium (size 8), 1 small (size 2)
- Watercolour pan paints – cobalt blue, raw sienna, burnt sienna, burnt umber, raw umber
- Old toothbrush
- Masking fluid
- Water container

1 *The first stage of this painting was to dip an old toothbrush into a saucer of masking fluid and flick the fluid up across the paper following the direction of the water spray.*

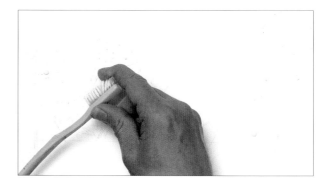

2 *Once this had dried, I applied an underwash of raw sienna to wet paper with a large brush. INSET: While this was still damp, I flooded burnt umber and cobalt blue mixes onto the darkest rocks.*

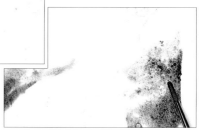

3 The grass area of the water's edge was painted onto the raw sienna underwash, and I created a little definition by drawing onto the rock shapes with a small brush and a very dark tone.

4 Using a small brush I added texture to the rocks by dropping pure earth colours onto wet paint, one after the other in rapid succession. This allowed the paint to create its own mixes, which dried at different speeds, creating a sense of texture.

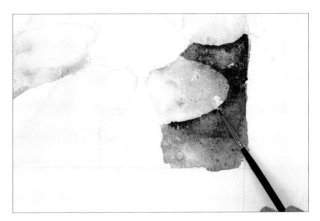

5 This process was continued across the rocks, where I worked carefully around the white sections of water. INSET: I applied burnt sienna, raw sienna and raw umber wet, and allowed them to dry unevenly.

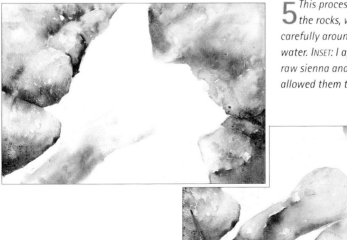

6 *Moving on to the rocks in the middle, I added a little Cobalt blue to darken the tones, ensuring that the darkest sections were those low down at the waterline.*

7 *Working carefully, I added texture to all the rocks, and I then used a small brush to sharpen up any lines or ridges with the darkest of colour mixes.*

8 *For the water, I used a small brush and very diluted versions of the rock colours already in the palette to paint some of the areas of rock visible through the water.*

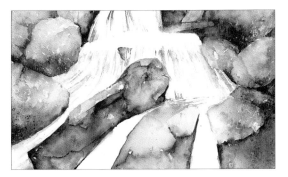

9 Working downwards, I carefully followed the direction of the flow of the water around and across the rocks. The less paper I applied paint to, the faster the water appeared to be flowing.

10 The water in the immediate centre foreground was the darkest as it flowed underneath an overhanging boulder – I made confident one-stroke applications with a small brush using the darkest of tones.

11 Once all the paint had thoroughly dried, I removed the initial spattering of masking fluid by gently rubbing over the surface of the picture with a putty rubber. It's worth restating that the paint must be completely dry, otherwise the rubber will smear it.

12 The final stage of this painting involved using a small brush to sharpen up the edges on a few boulders, carefully avoiding any of the pure white paper that I had revealed by removing the masking fluid.

ENERGY

The feeling of power, energy and movement in this painting is largely the result of a vigorous application of masking fluid to create the spray, and strong, directional brushstrokes along the line of the water flow. The close-up framing of the picture also contributes to the sense of movement that is present within the scene.

The darkest tones and rock detail are drawn onto the underwash with a small brush.

Directionally spraying masking fluid helps to establish a feeling of movement and energy.

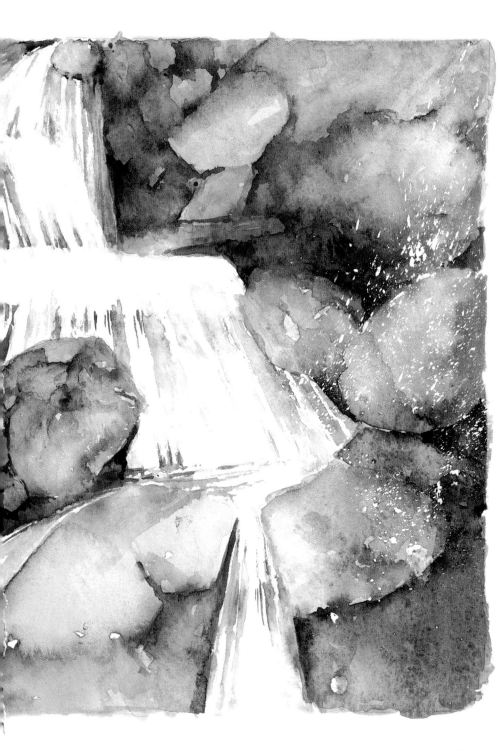

INDEX